11+
NON-VERBAL REASONING

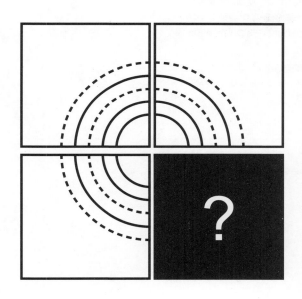

Ages 9–10

Practice

Series editor Tracey Phelps,
the 11+ tutor with a

96% PASS RATE

■SCHOLASTIC

Published in the UK by Scholastic, 2021

Book End, Range Road, Witney, Oxfordshire, OX29 0YD

Scholastic Ireland, 89E Lagan Road, Dublin Industrial Estate, Glasnevin, Dublin, D11 HP5F

www.scholastic.co.uk

© 2021 Scholastic Limited

1 2 3 4 5 6 7 8 9 1 2 3 4 5 6 7 8 9 0

A CIP catalogue record for this book is available from the British Library.
ISBN 978-1407-19024-2

Printed and bound by Replika Press Pvt. Ltd.

Paper made from wood grown in sustainable forests and other controlled sources.

Author
Tracey Phelps

Editorial team
Rachel Morgan, Vicki Yates, Sarah Davies, Julia Roberts,

Design team
Dipa Mistry and Andrea Lewis

Illustrations
Tracey Phelps

Contents

About the CEM test and this book

About the CEM test

The Centre for Evaluation and Monitoring (CEM) is one of the leading providers of the tests that grammar schools use in selecting students at 11+. The CEM test assesses a student's ability in Verbal Reasoning, Non-verbal Reasoning, English and Mathematics. Pupils typically take the CEM test at the start of Year 6.

Students answer multiple-choice questions and record their answers on a separate answer sheet. This answer sheet is then marked via OMR (Optical Mark Recognition) scanning technology.

The content and question types may vary slightly each year. The English and Verbal Reasoning components have included synonyms, antonyms, word associations, shuffled sentences, cloze (gap fill) passages and comprehension questions.

The Mathematics and Non-verbal Reasoning components span the Key Stage 2 Mathematics curriculum, with emphasis on worded problems. It is useful to note that the CEM test may include mathematics topics introduced at Year 6, such as ratio, proportion and probability.

The other main provider of such tests is GL Assessment. The GLA test assesses the same subjects as the CEM test and uses a multiple-choice format.

About this book

Scholastic 11+ Non-Verbal Reasoning for the CEM test (ages 9–10) is part of the Pass Your 11+ series and offers authentic multiple-choice practice activities.

This book offers:

- Targeted practice and opportunities for children to test their understanding and develop their non-verbal reasoning skills.
- Opportunities to master different question types, including cubes, rotation, hidden shapes sequences, grids and more.
- Multiple-choice questions that reflect the different question types that are common in the CEM 11+ test, at a level appropriate for the age group.
- Short answers at the end of the book.
- Extended answers online with useful explanations at
  www.scholastic.co.uk/pass-your-11-plus/extras or via the QR code.

How to use this book?

It is suggested that your child focuses on one question type at a time and that they allow 20 minutes to answer all the questions in that section. As your child becomes more proficient at doing these types of questions, reduce the time allowed but expect the same number of questions to be covered in order to practise working at speed.

Your child's scores in each section will allow you to see where their strengths lie and areas where they might need more practice in the future.

Odd one out

Which is the odd one out? Circle one of the options A to E.
The answer to the example is E as it is the only shape to have curved lines.

Example

A   B   C   D   Ⓔ

1

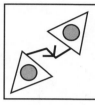 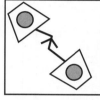 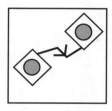 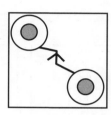 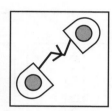

A   B   C   D   E

2

A   B   C   D   E

3

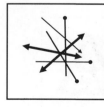 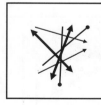 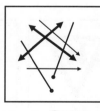 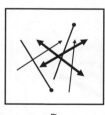 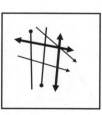

A   B   C   D   E

4

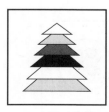    

A   B   C   D   E

5

A B C D E

6

A B C D E

7

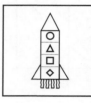    

A B C D E

8

A B C D E

9

A B C D E

10

A B C D E

Odd one out

11

A B C D E

12

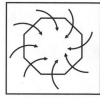  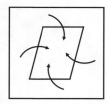 

A B C D E

13

A B C D E

14

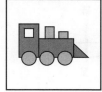   

A B C D E

15

 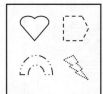   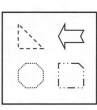

A B C D E

16

A B C D E

17

A　　　　　　B　　　　　　C　　　　　　D　　　　　　E

18

   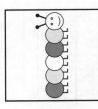 

A　　　　　　B　　　　　　C　　　　　　D　　　　　　E

19

A　　　　　　B　　　　　　C　　　　　　D　　　　　　E

20

  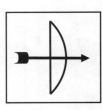 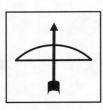 

A　　　　　　B　　　　　　C　　　　　　D　　　　　　E

21

 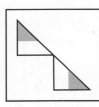 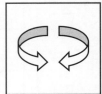  

A　　　　　　B　　　　　　C　　　　　　D　　　　　　E

22

   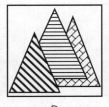 

A　　　　　　B　　　　　　C　　　　　　D　　　　　　E

Views

Which 2D plan matches the 3D view (either top-down or side view) of the picture on the left? Circle one of the options A to D.

The answer to the example is C as it is the view of the shape from above.

Example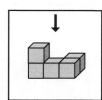

   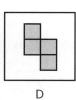

A   B   Ⓒ   D

---

1 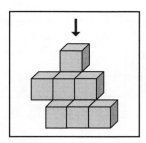

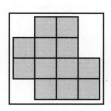 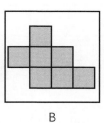 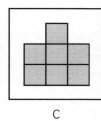 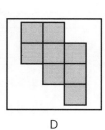

A   B   C   D

---

2 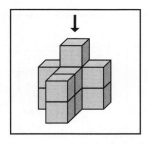

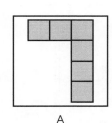 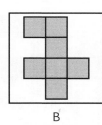 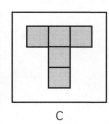 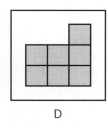

A   B   C   D

---

3 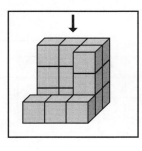

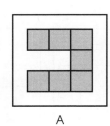 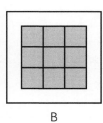 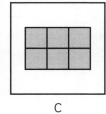 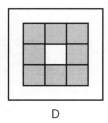

A   B   C   D

---

4 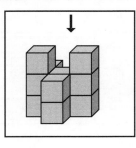

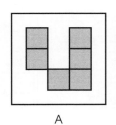 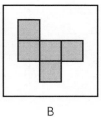 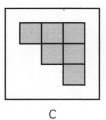 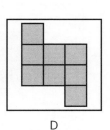

A   B   C   D

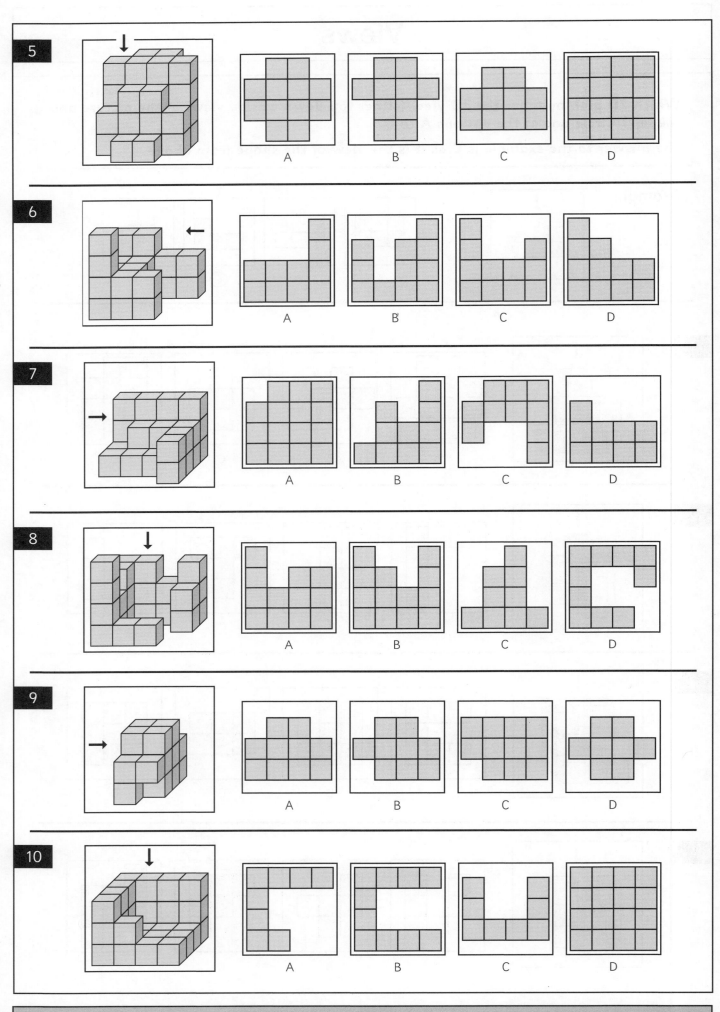

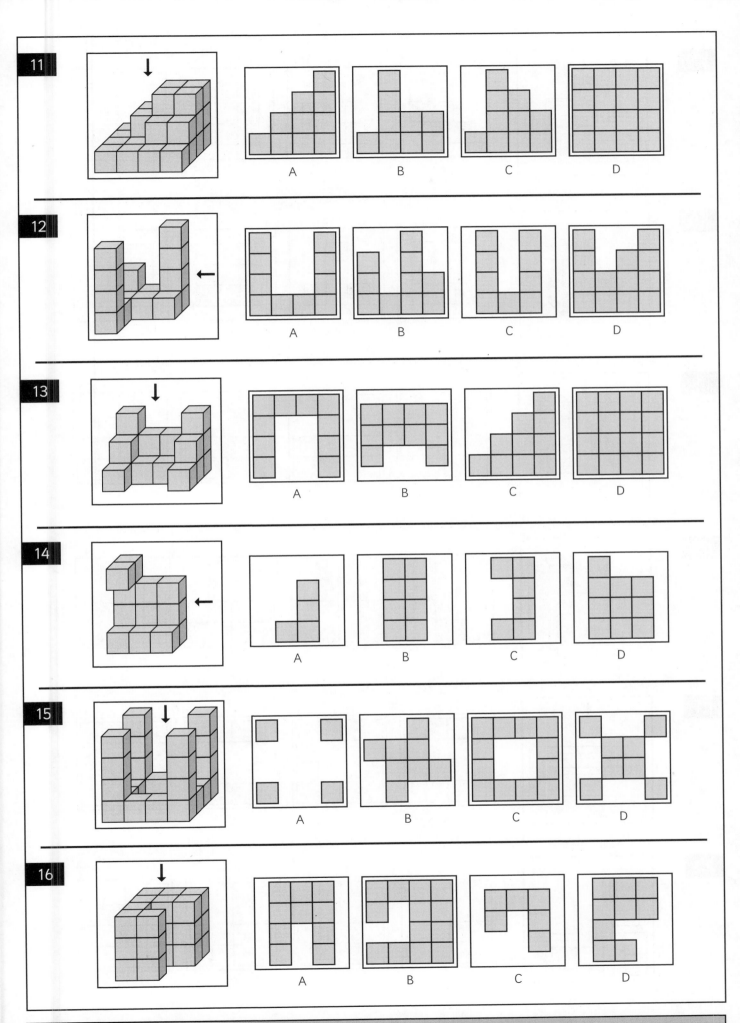

11

12

13

14

15

16

A   B   C   D

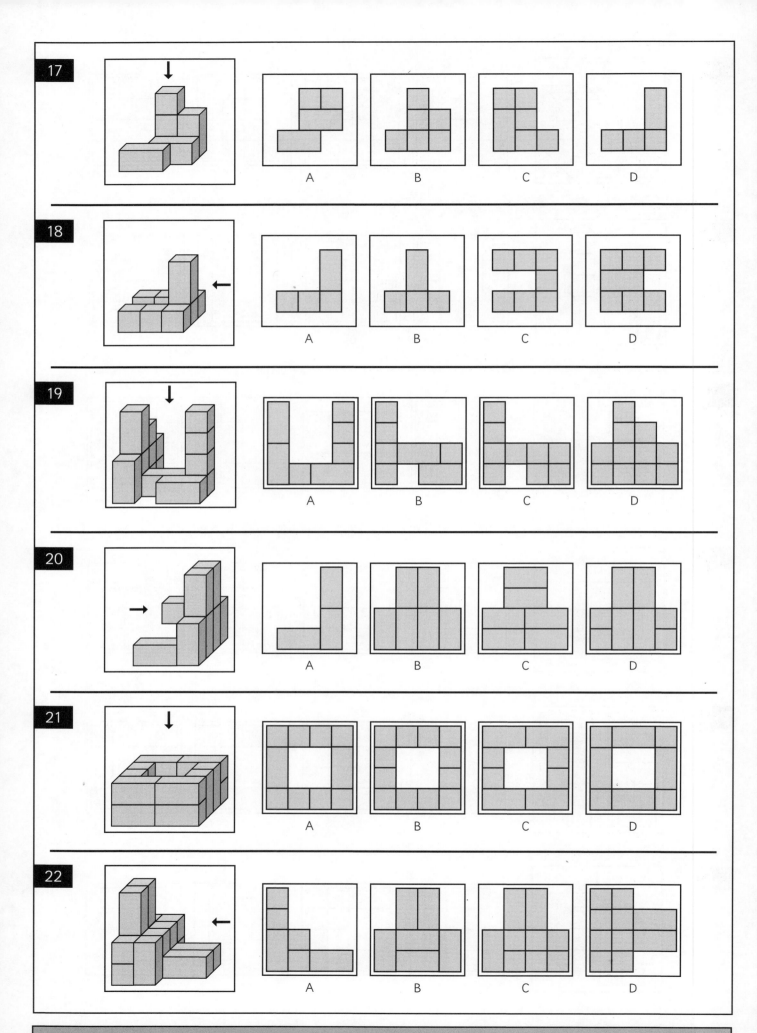

Grids

Find the correct shape to complete each matrix. Circle one of the options A to E.

The answer to the example is A as the shape has been rotated 45 degrees clockwise.

Example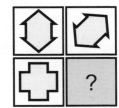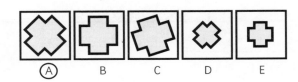

1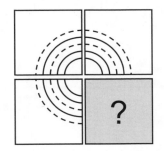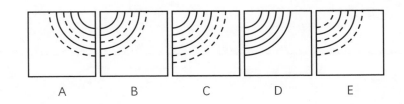

2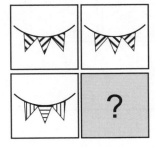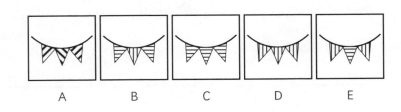

3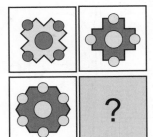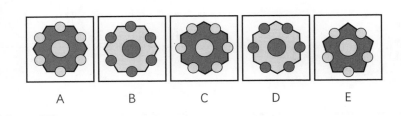

4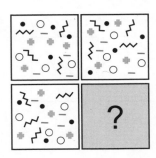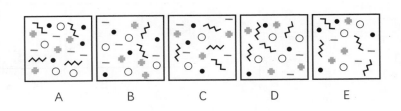

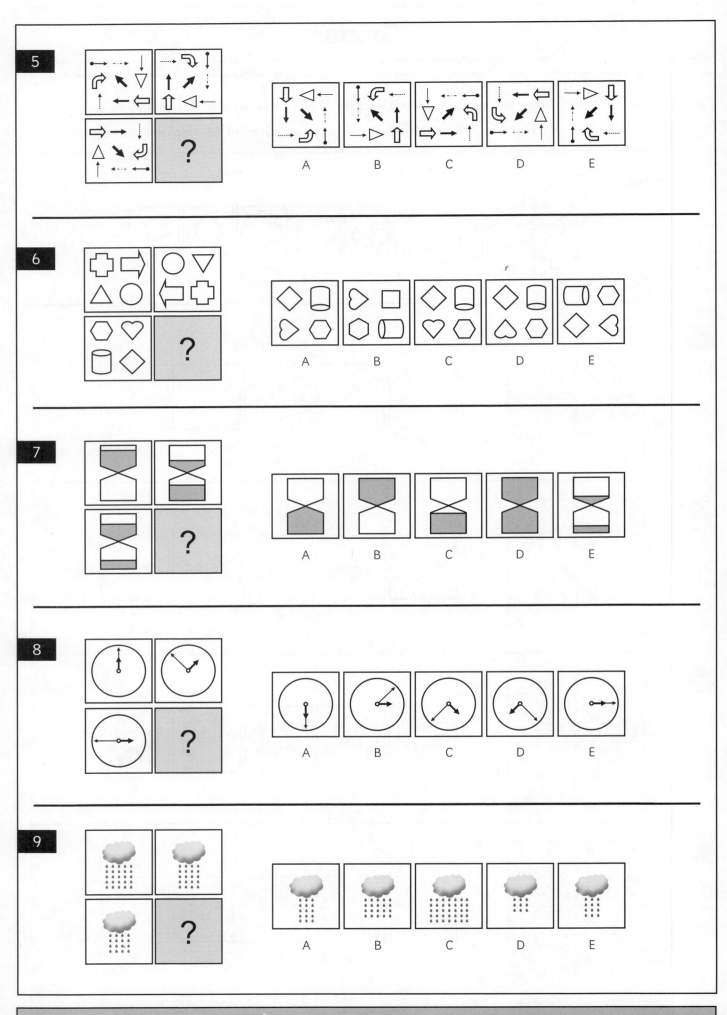

10

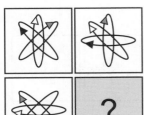
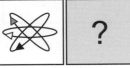

A   B   C   D   E

11

A   B   C   D   E

12

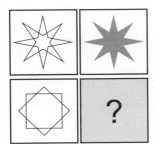

A   B   C   D   E

13

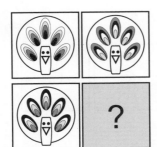

A   B   C   D   E

14

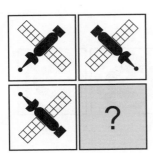

A   B   C   D   E

15

A   B   C   D   E

16

A   B   C   D   E

17

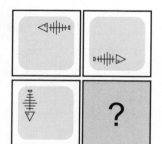

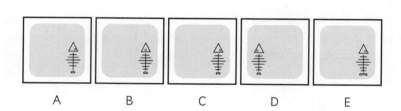

A   B   C   D   E

18

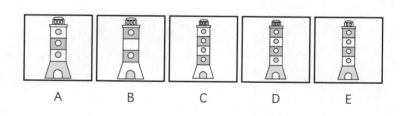

A   B   C   D   E

19

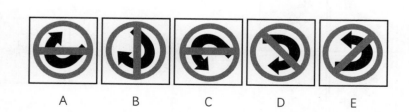

A   B   C   D   E

20

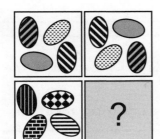

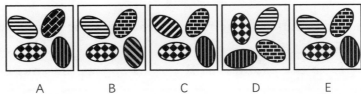

A B C D E

21

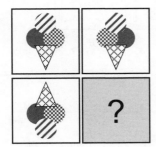

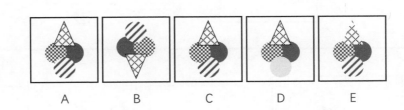

A B C D E

22

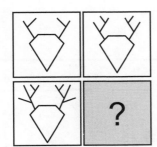

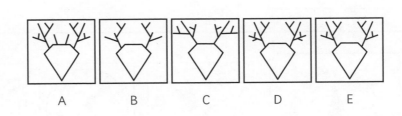

A B C D E

23

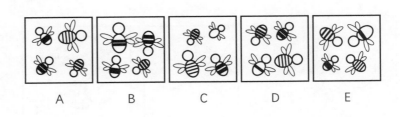

A B C D E

24

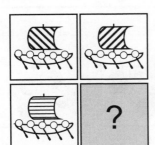

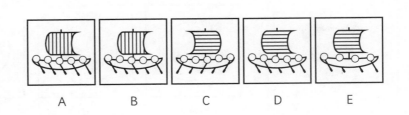

A B C D E

Rotations

Find the shape that can be rotated to make the figure on the left. Circle one of the options A to D.

The answer to the example is B as this shows the shape on the left after rotation.

Example

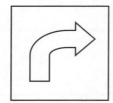

A   Ⓑ   C   D

1

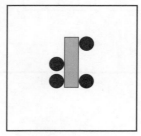   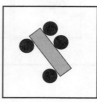

A   B   C   D

2

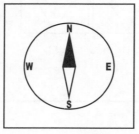  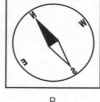 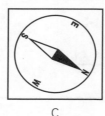 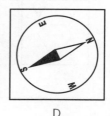

A   B   C   D

3

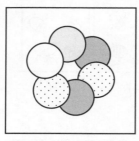 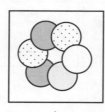 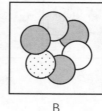 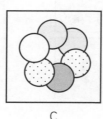 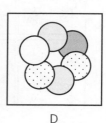

A   B   C   D

4

A   B   C   D

5

A B C D

6

 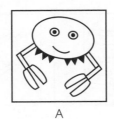   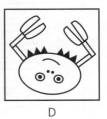

A B C D

7

A B C D

8

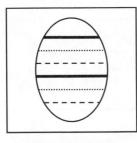 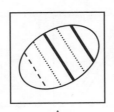 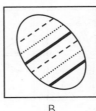 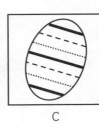 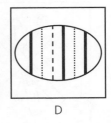

A B C D

9

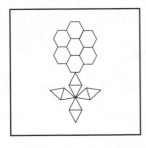 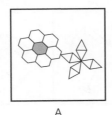 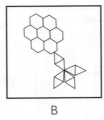 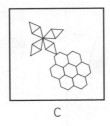 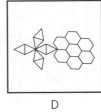

A B C D

10

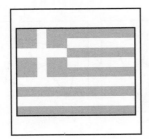 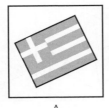   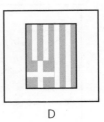

A B C D

11

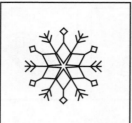

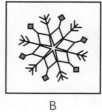

A   B   C   D

12

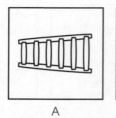

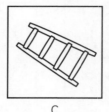

A   B   C   D

13

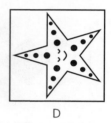

A   B   C   D

14

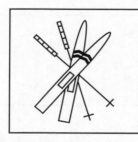
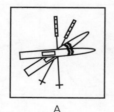
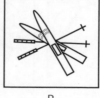
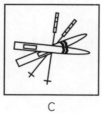
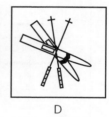

A   B   C   D

15

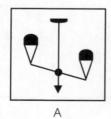

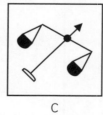
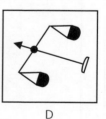

A   B   C   D

16

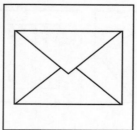

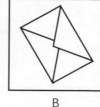
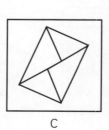
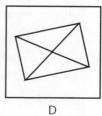

A   B   C   D

17

A   B   C   D

18

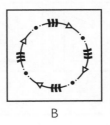

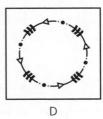

A   B   C   D

19

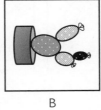

A   B   C   D

20

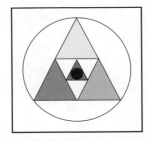
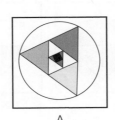
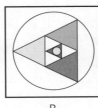
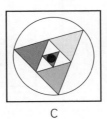
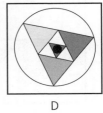

A   B   C   D

21

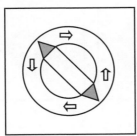
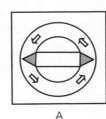
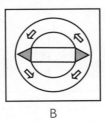
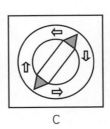
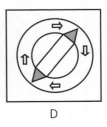

A   B   C   D

22

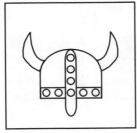
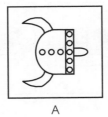

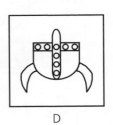

A   B   C   D

Reflections

Find the shape that is formed when the shape in the left box is reflected. Circle one of the options A to D.

The answer to the example is **D** as the shape is a reflection of the shape on the left.

Example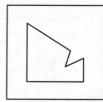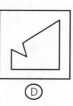

A   B   C   Ⓓ

1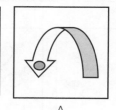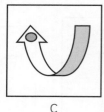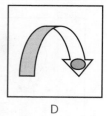

A   B   C   D

2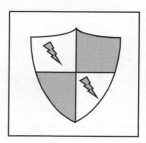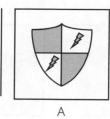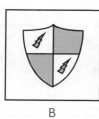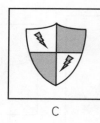

A   B   C   D

3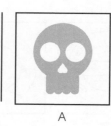

A   B   C   D

4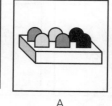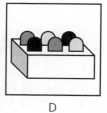

A   B   C   D

5

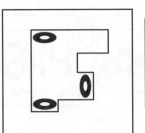

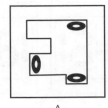
A

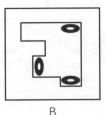
B

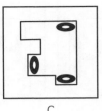
C

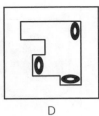
D

6

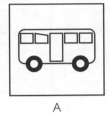
A

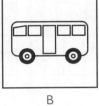
B

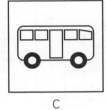
C

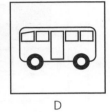
D

7

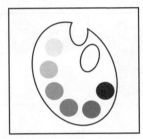

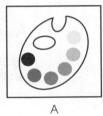
A

B

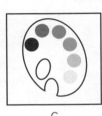
C

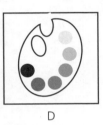
D

8

A

B

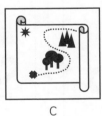
C

D

9

A

B

C

D

10

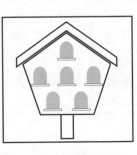

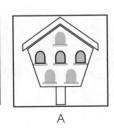
A

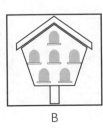
B

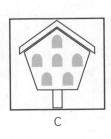
C

D

11

A

B

C

D

12

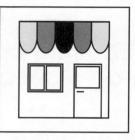

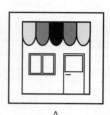

A

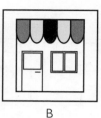

B

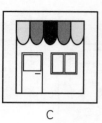

C

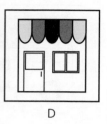

D

13

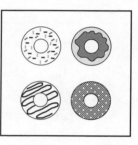

A

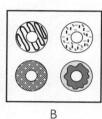

B

C

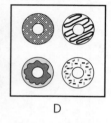

D

14

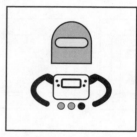

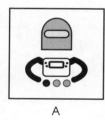

A

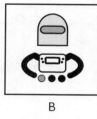

B

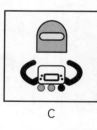

C

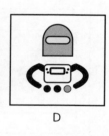

D

15

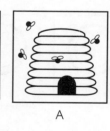

A

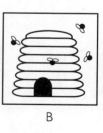

B

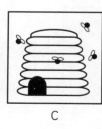

C

D

16

A

B

C

D

17

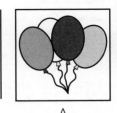
A

B

C

D

18

A

B

C

D

19

A

B

C

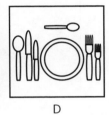
D

20

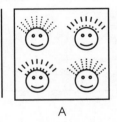
A

B

C

D

21

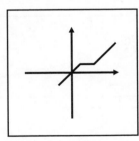

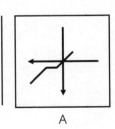
A

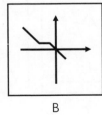
B

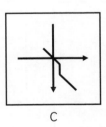
C

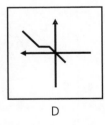
D

22

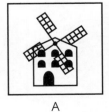
A

B

C

D

Hidden shapes

Identify which of the options contains the shape on the left. Circle one of the options A to D. The answer to the example is D as this contains the shape on the left.

Example

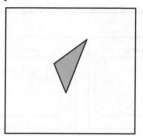 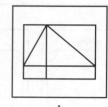 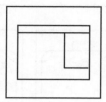 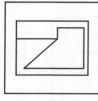 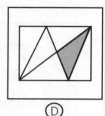

A   B   C   D

1

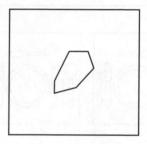 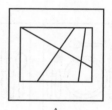 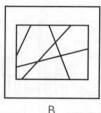 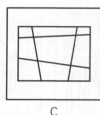 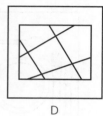

A   B   C   D

2

 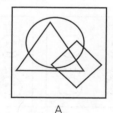 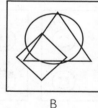  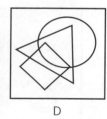

A   B   C   D

3

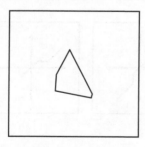 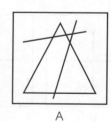   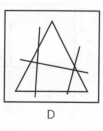

A   B   C   D

4

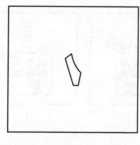 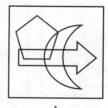   

A   B   C   D

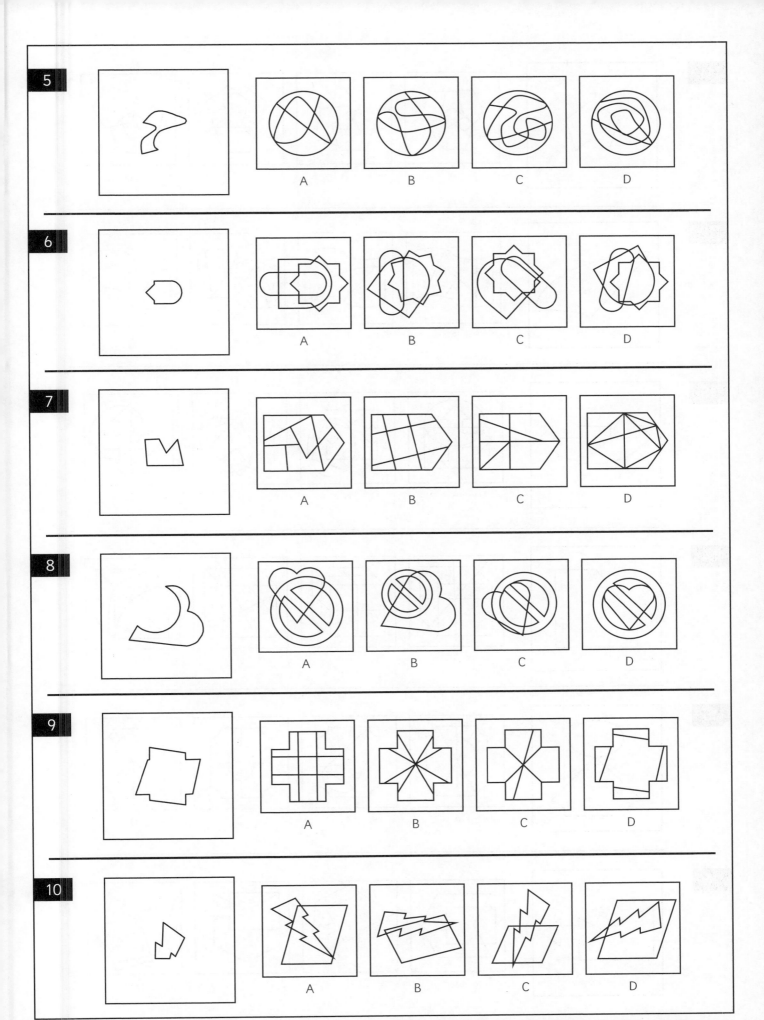

5   A   B   C   D

6   A   B   C   D

7   A   B   C   D

8   A   B   C   D

9   A   B   C   D

10   A   B   C   D

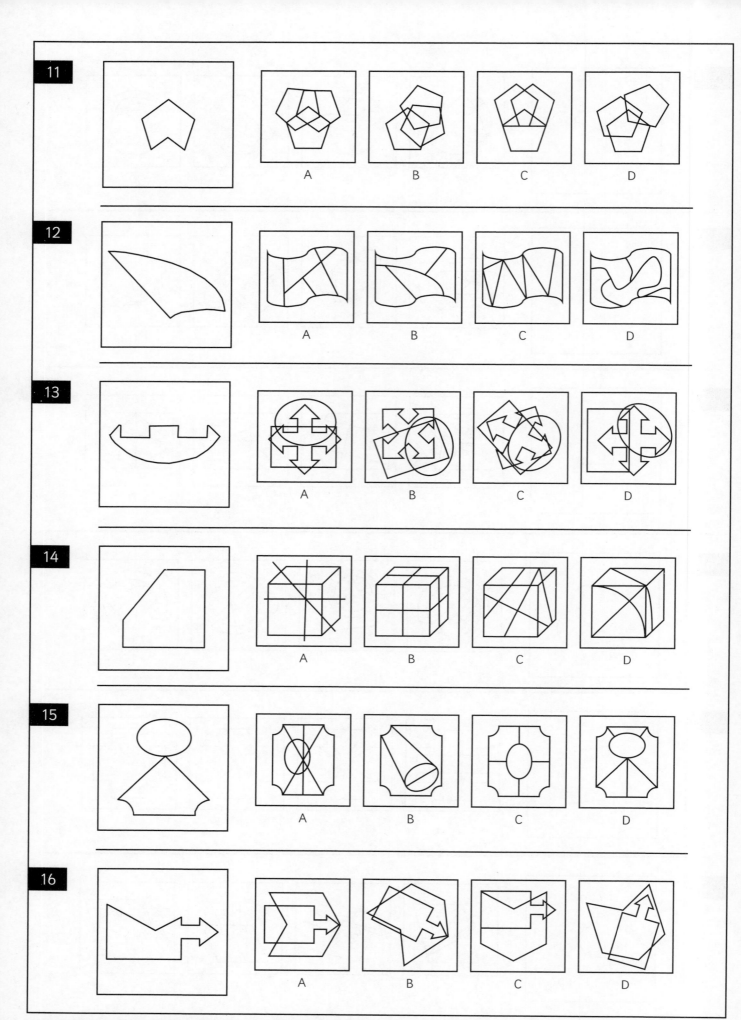

11

A B C D

12

A B C D

13

A B C D

14

A B C D

15

A B C D

16

A B C D

17

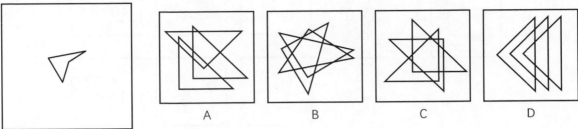

A   B   C   D

18

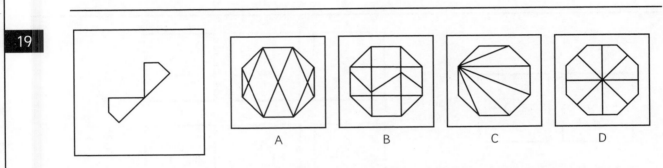

A   B   C   D

19

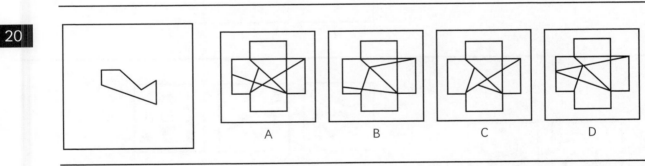

A   B   C   D

20

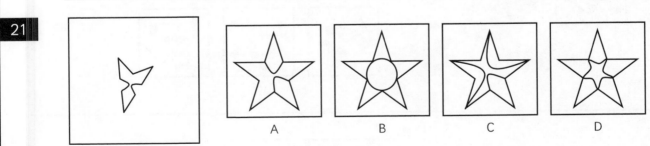

A   B   C   D

21

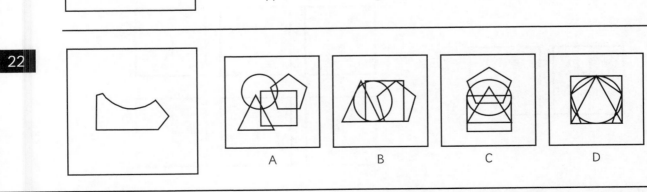

A   B   C   D

22

A   B   C   D

Families

Choose the option which is most like the two pictures on the left. Circle one of the options A to F. The answer to the example is E, as both pictures have three identical shapes of three differing sizes with the largest shape in the foreground.

Example

A B C

D Ⓔ F

1

A B C

D E F

2

A B C

D E F

3

A B C

D E F

4

A

B

C

D

E

F

5

A

B

C

D

E

F

6

A

B

C

D

E

F

7

A

B

C

D

E

F

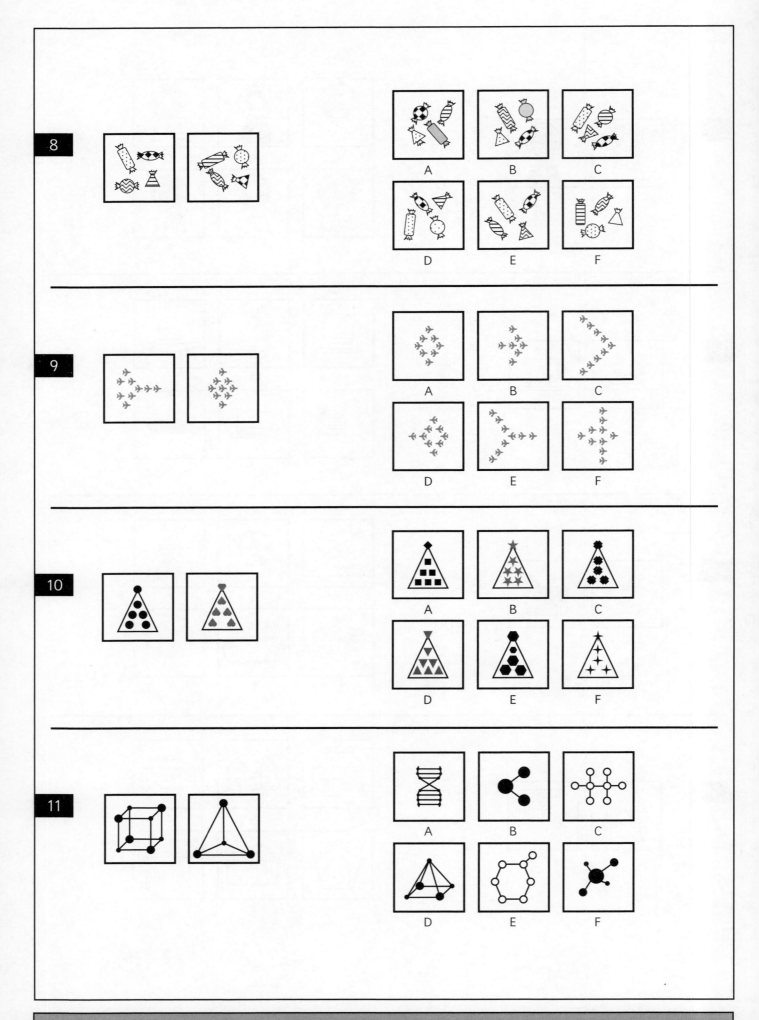

12

A	B	C
D	E	F

13

A	B	C
D	E	F

14

A	B	C
D	E	F

15

A	B	C
D	E	F

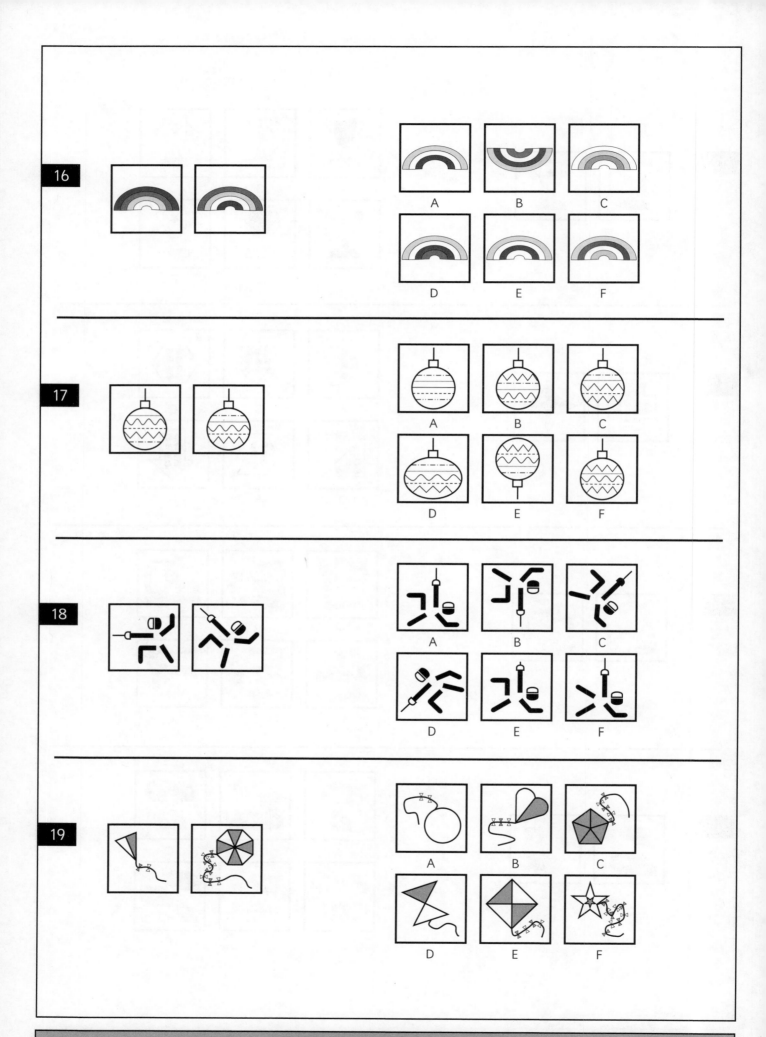

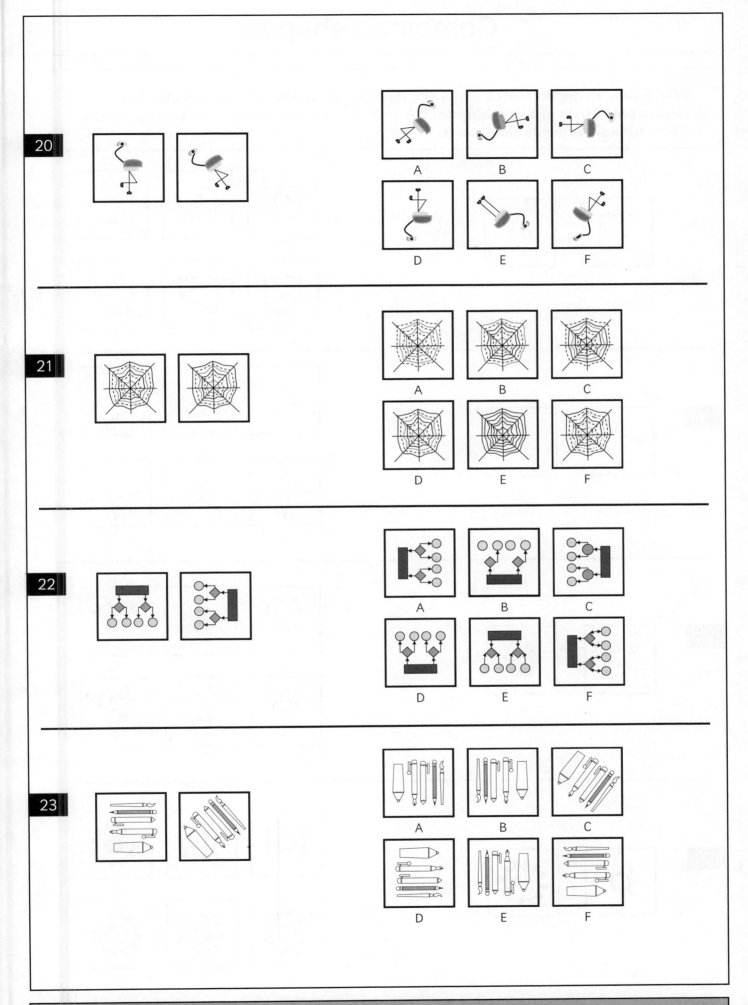

Combined shapes

Which new shape is created when the two shapes on the left are combined or subtracted? Circle one of the options A to F. The answer to the example is A as the white triangle is inside the square.

Example

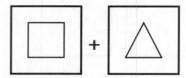

(A)

B

C

D

E

F

1

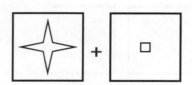

A

B

C

D

E

F

2

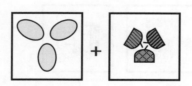

A

B

C

D

E

F

3

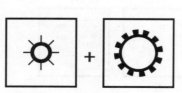

A

B

C

D

E

F

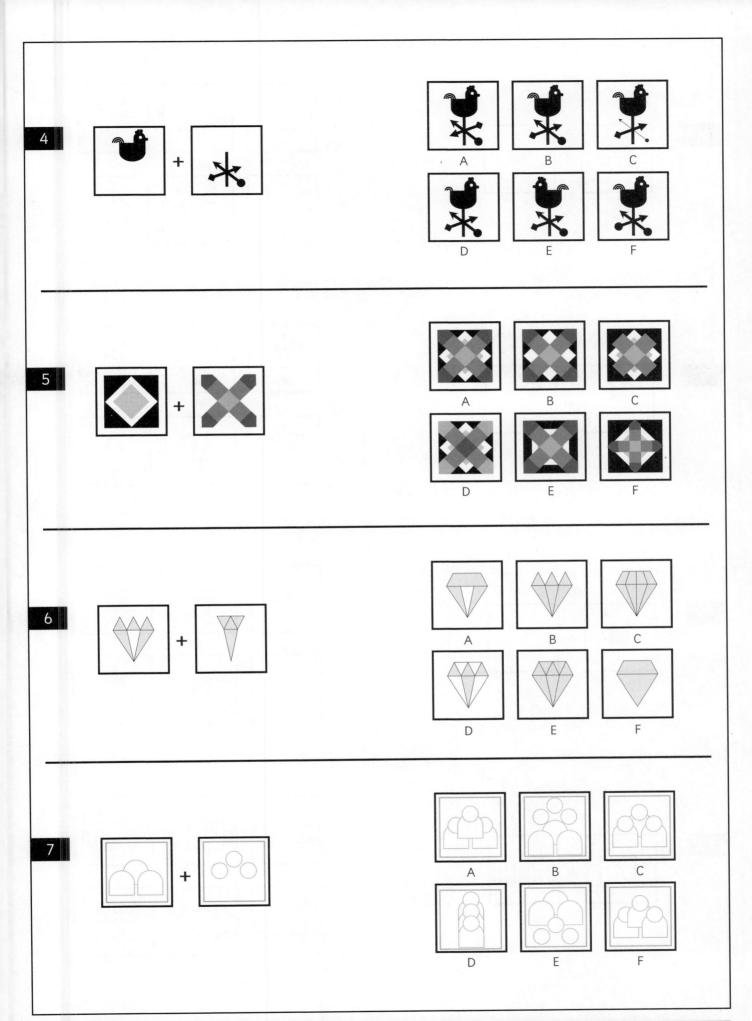

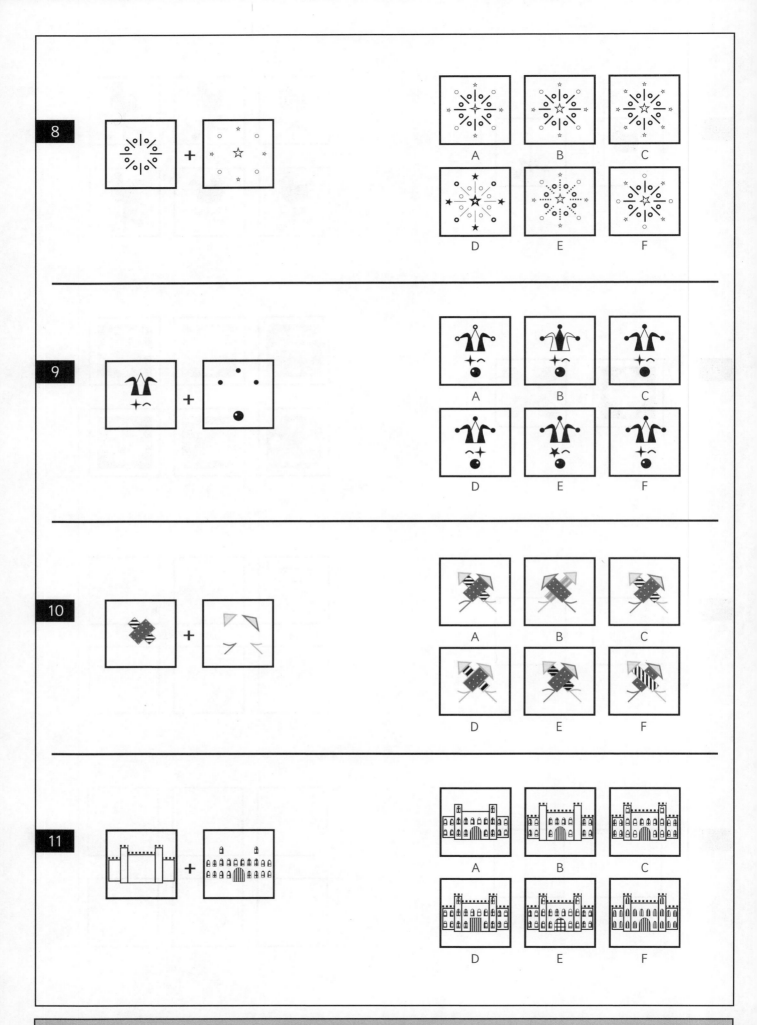

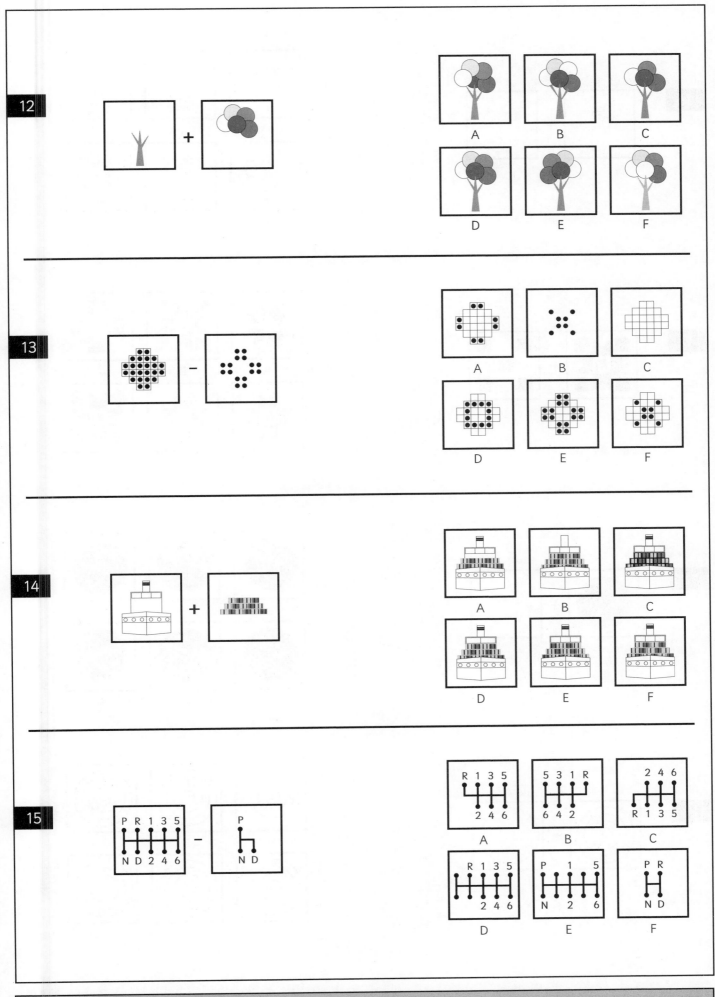

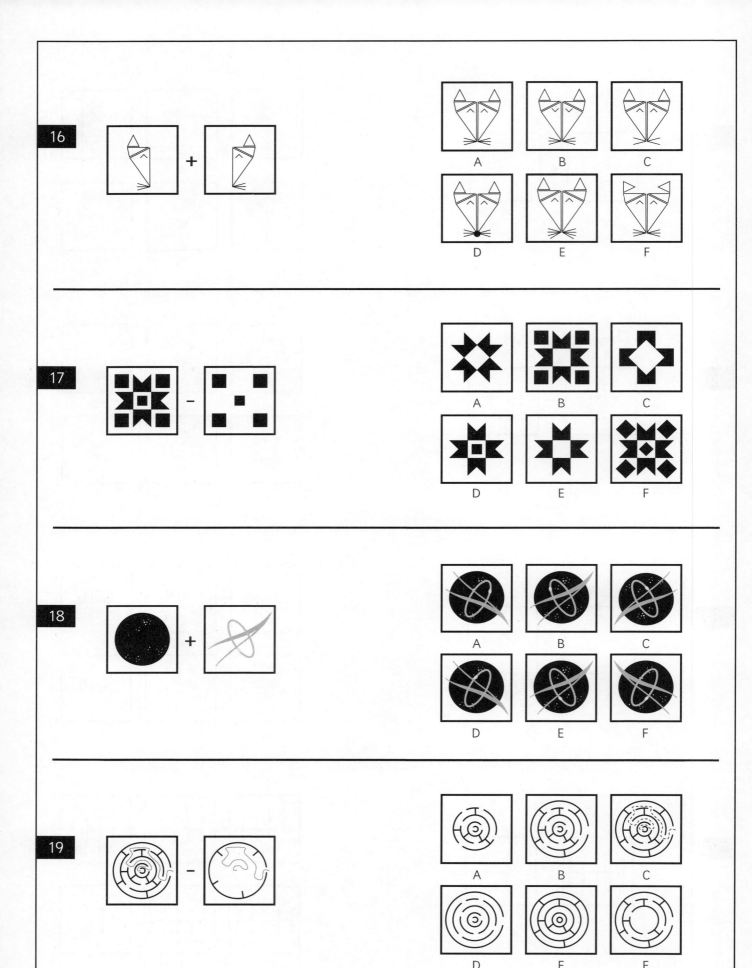

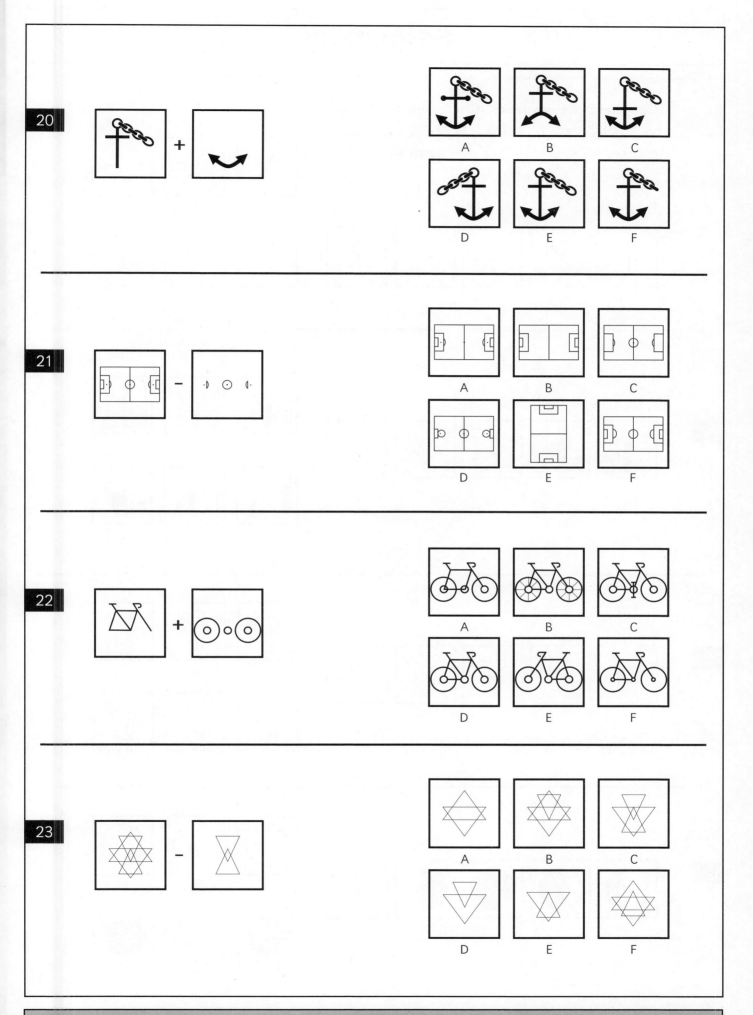

Sequences

Complete the sequence. Circle one of the options A to F.

The answer in the example is **D** as the shape rotates 45 degrees clockwise each time.

Example

A

B

C

D

E

F

1

A

B

C

D

E

F

2

A

B

C

D

E

F

3

A

B

C

D

E

F

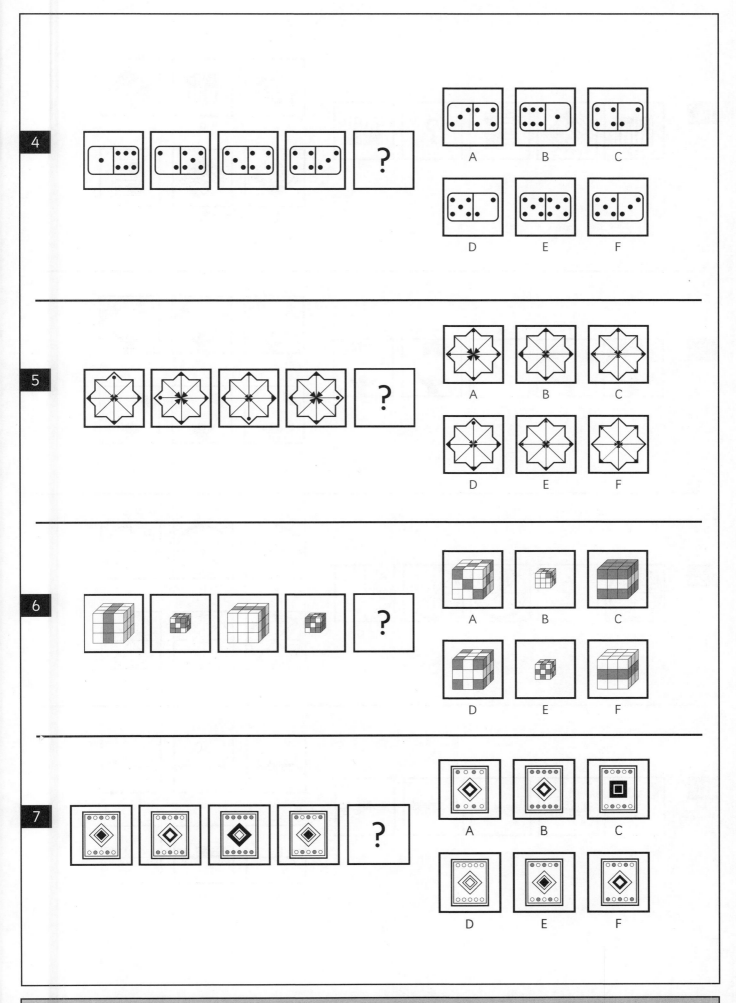

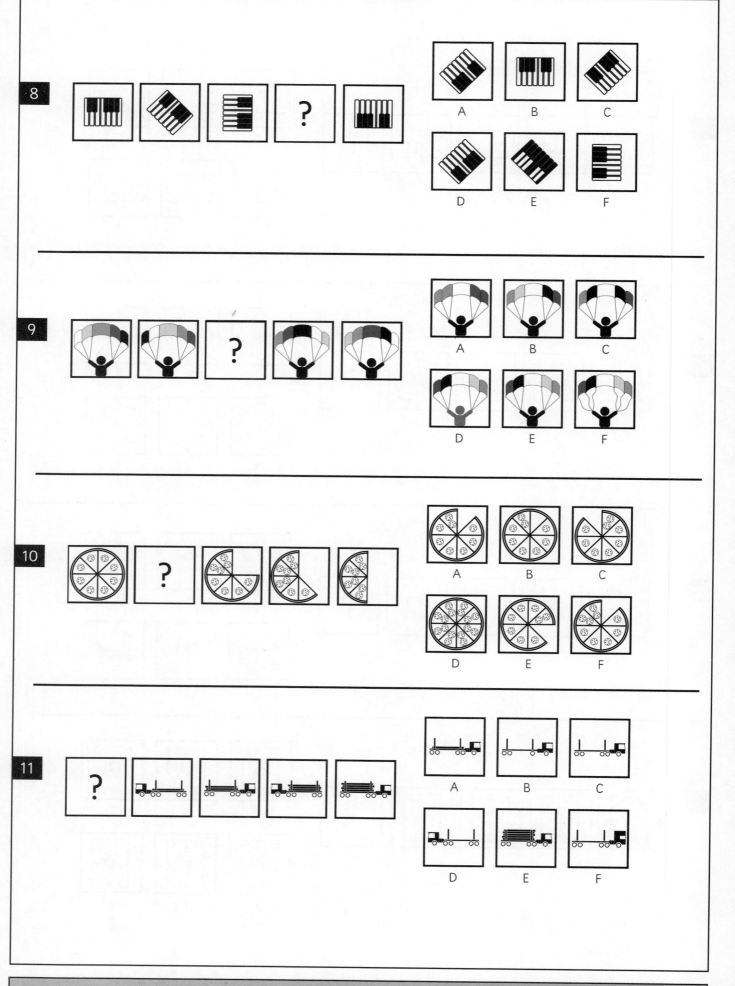

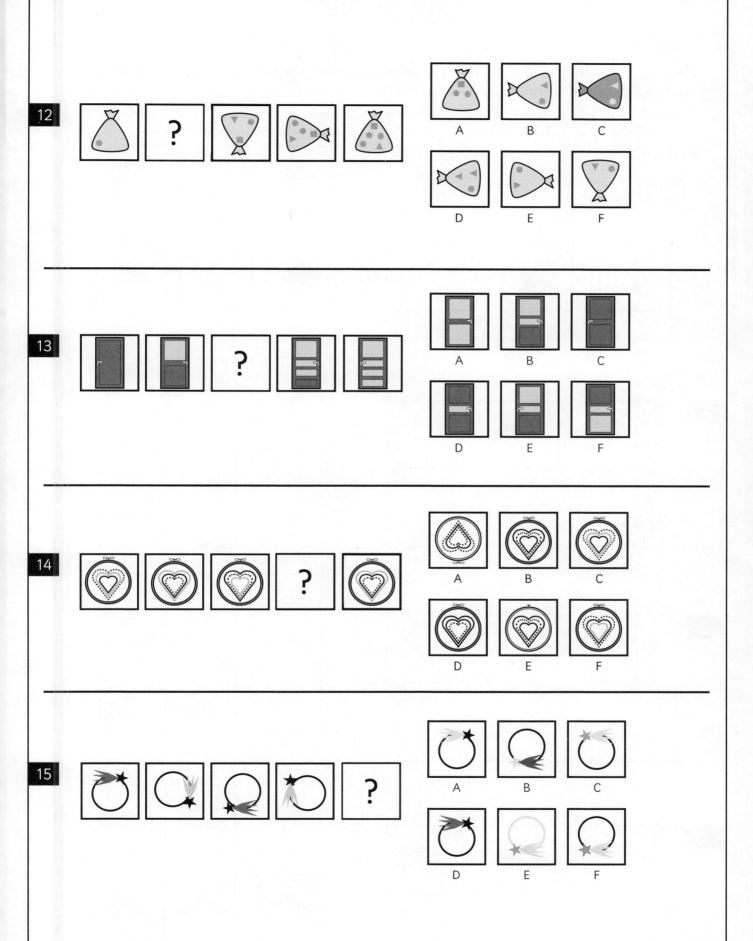

Analogies

The first two pictures on the left are related to each other in some way. Decide which picture is related to the third picture in the same way.

Circle one of the options A to F. The answer to the example is A.

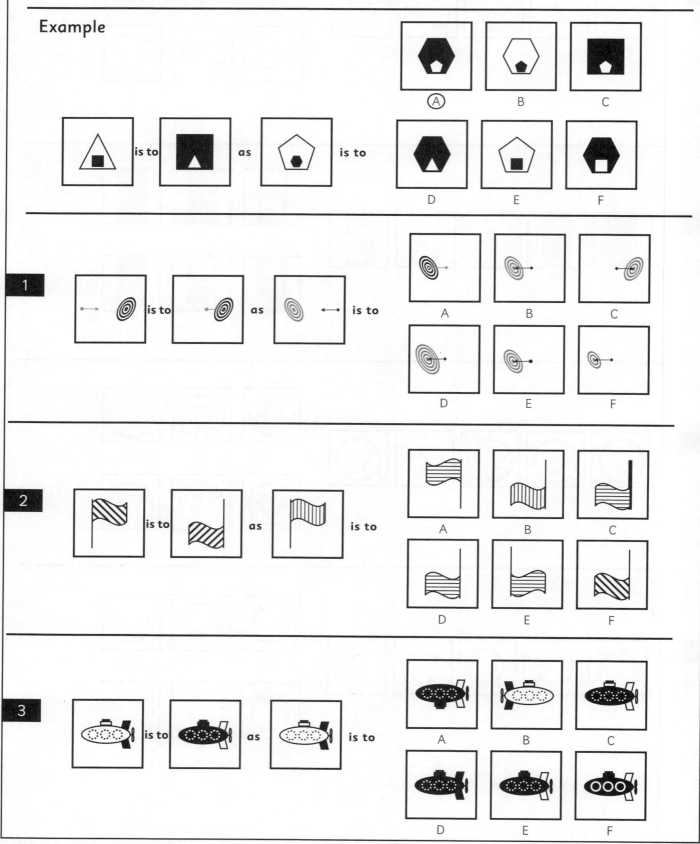

Example

1

2

3

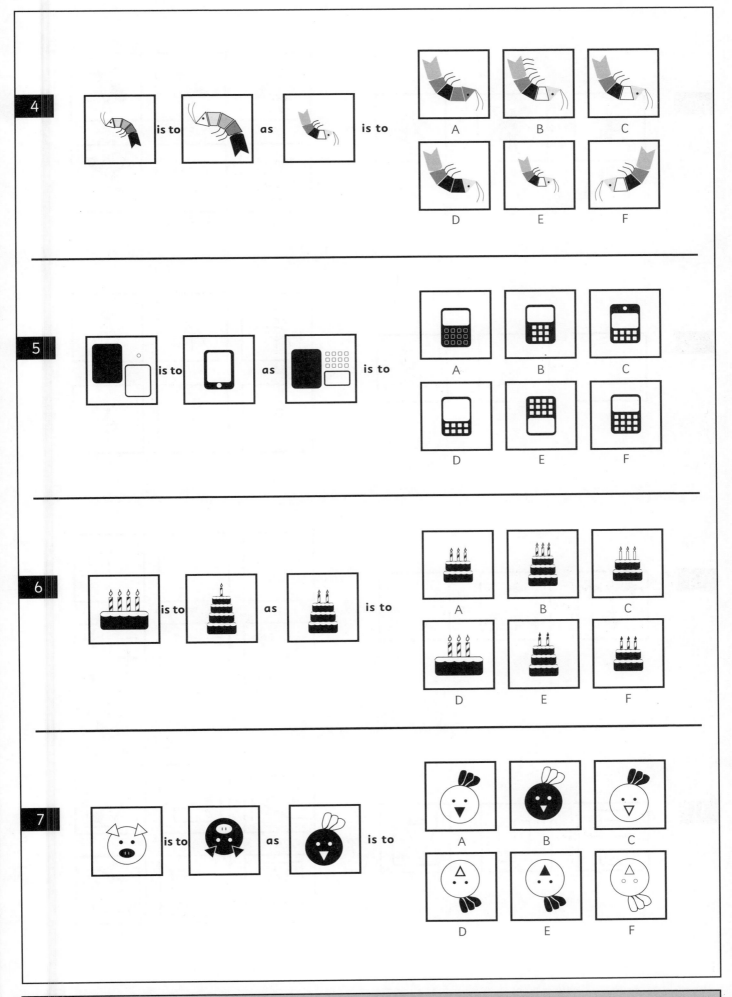

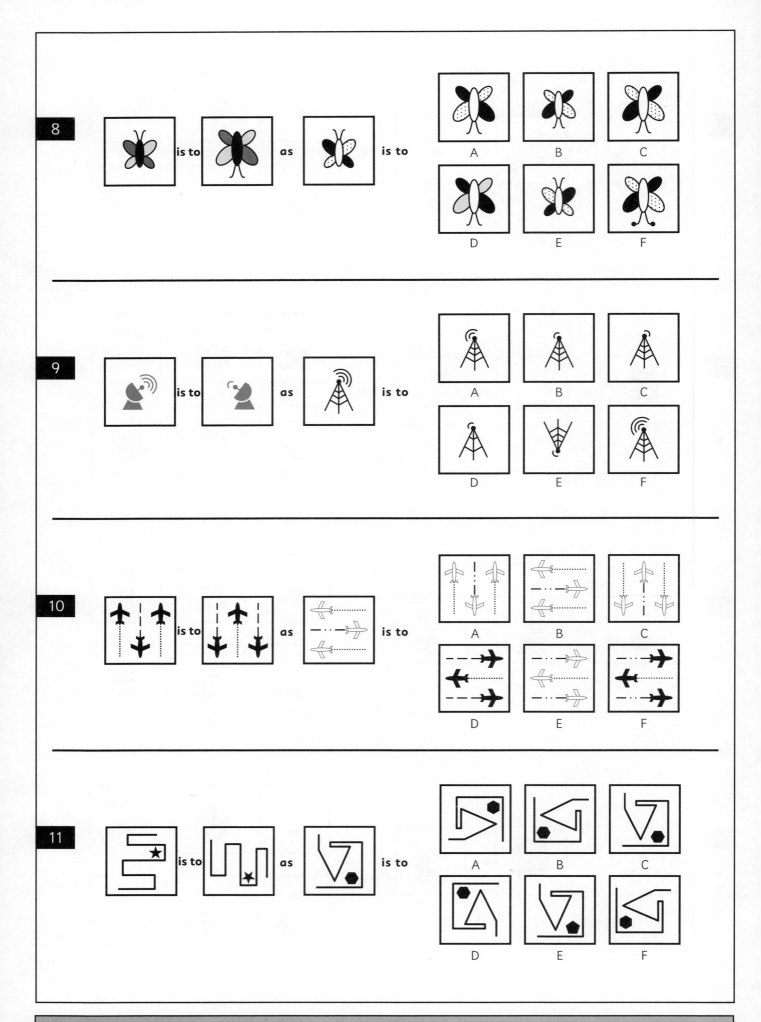

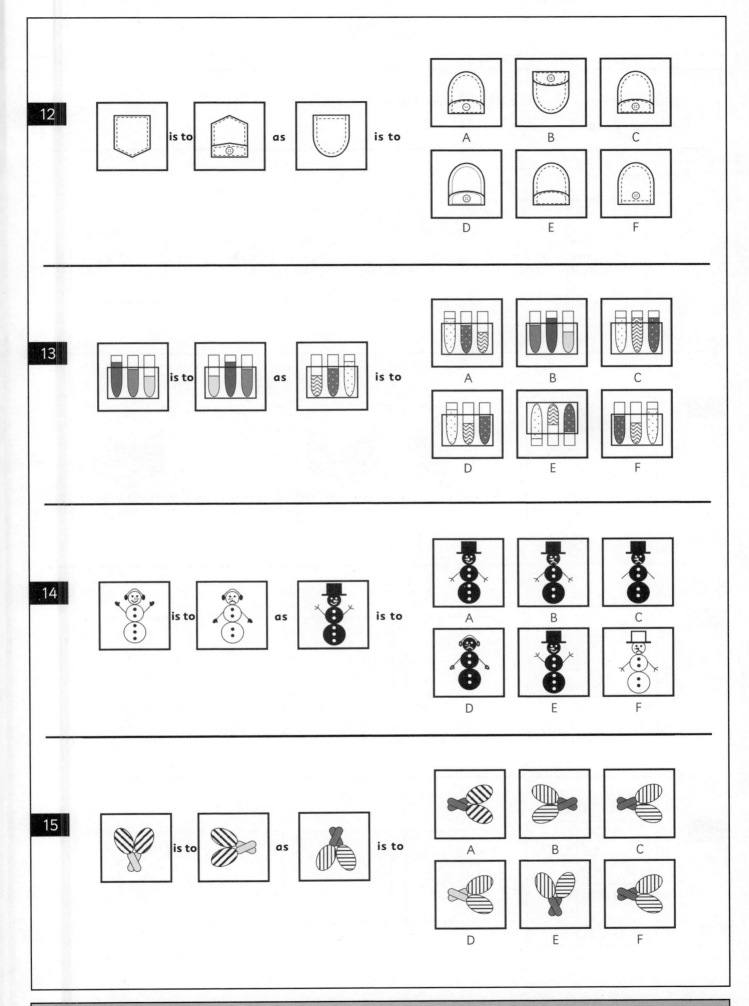

Cubes

Which cube matches the net? Circle one of the options A to D.

The answer to the example is D.

Example

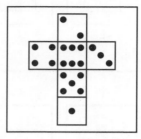 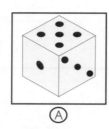 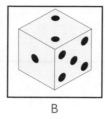 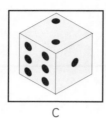 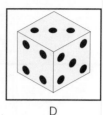

(A) B C D

1

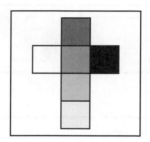   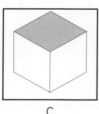 

A B C D

2

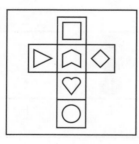 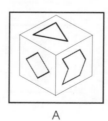 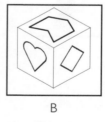  

A B C D

3

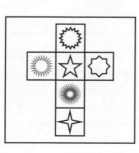 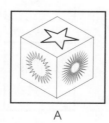 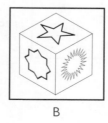 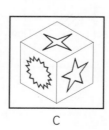 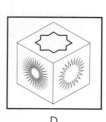

A B C D

Cubes

4

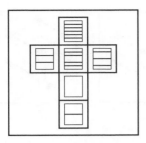
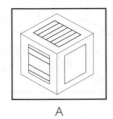

A   B   C   D

5

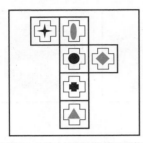
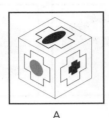
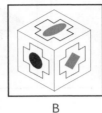
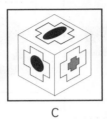
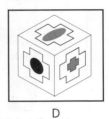

A   B   C   D

6

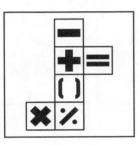

A   B   C   D

7

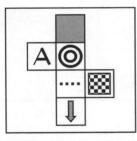
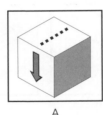

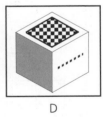

A   B   C   D

8

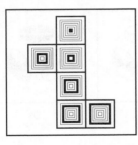
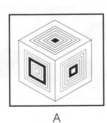
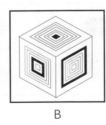
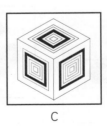

A   B   C   D

9

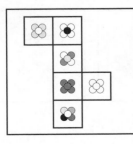
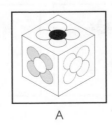
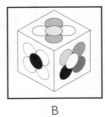
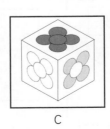
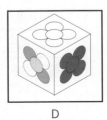

A   B   C   D

10

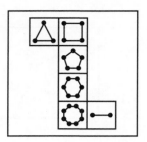
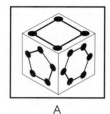
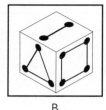
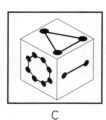
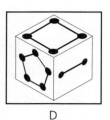

| A | B | C | D |

11

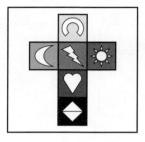

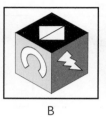

| A | B | C | D |

.12

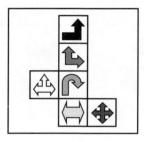

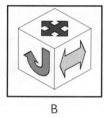

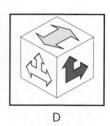

| A | B | C | D |

13

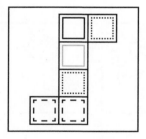
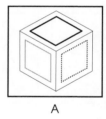
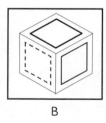
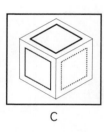
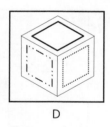

| A | B | C | D |

14

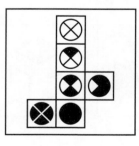

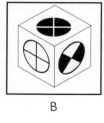

| A | B | C | D |

15

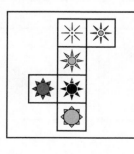
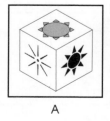
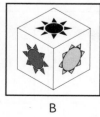
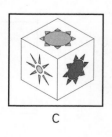

| A | B | C | D |

Answers

Odd one out
pp.5–8

1	D
2	D
3	A
4	E
5	A
6	E
7	C
8	D
9	E
10	B
11	E
12	B
13	B
14	C
15	A
16	E
17	C
18	B
19	D
20	E
21	D
22	A

Views
pp.9–12

1	B
2	C
3	A
4	B
5	A
6	C
7	D
8	D
9	A
10	D
11	D
12	A
13	B
14	C
15	C
16	D
17	A
18	B
19	B
20	D
21	C
22	C

Grids
pp.13–17

1	B
2	B
3	D
4	A
5	E
6	D
7	C
8	C
9	E
10	A
11	A
12	B
13	C
14	E
15	B
16	C
17	C
18	D
19	D
20	E
21	A
22	E
23	A
24	B

Rotations
pp.18–21

1	D
2	A
3	A
4	B
5	D
6	B
7	C
8	B
9	C
10	D
11	A
12	D
13	D
14	A
15	C
16	B
17	A
18	B
19	B
20	C
21	C
22	D

Reflections
pp.22–25

1	C
2	A
3	A
4	C
5	B
6	D
7	D
8	B
9	A
10	B
11	A
12	C
13	C
14	A
15	B
16	D
17	D
18	C
19	B
20	D
21	D
22	A

Answers – Hidden shapes pp.26–29

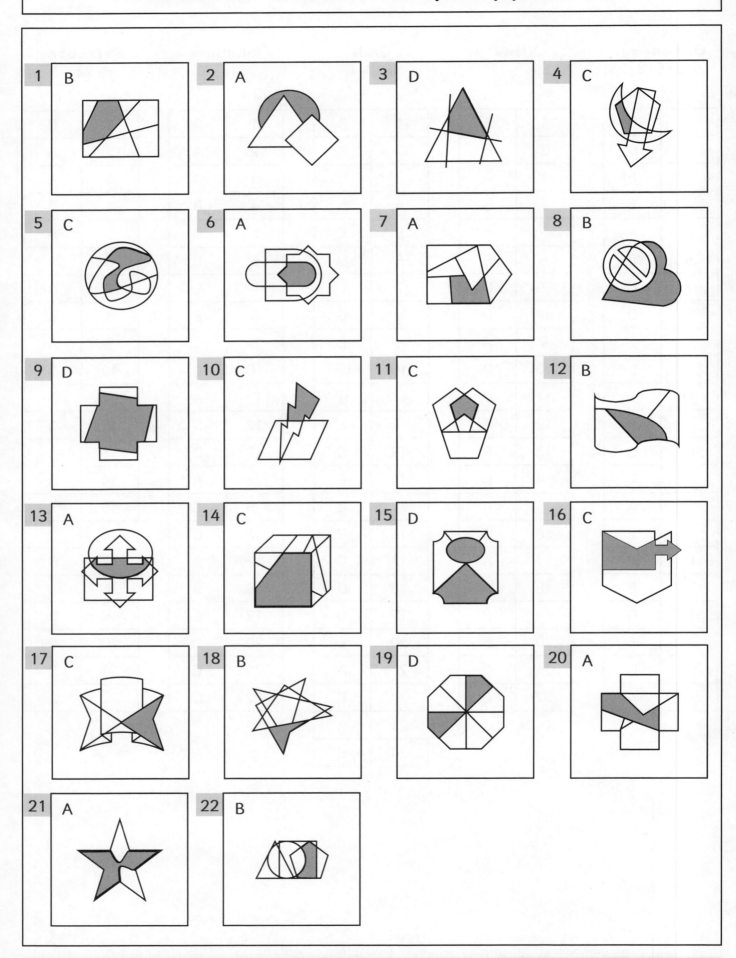

Answers

Families
pp.30–35

1	E
2	D
3	A
4	F
5	A
6	C
7	B
8	C
9	C
10	B
11	D
12	E
13	E
14	F
15	F
16	D
17	B
18	A
19	E
20	C
21	D
22	D
23	E

Combined shapes
pp.36–41

1	B
2	D
3	D
4	B
5	A
6	E
7	C
8	B
9	F
10	A
11	C
12	D
13	F
14	F
15	A
16	A
17	E
18	E
19	A
20	E
21	B
22	D
23	A

Sequences
pp.42–45

1	B
2	D
3	C
4	D
5	D
6	F
7	F
8	A
9	E
10	A
11	C
12	B
13	E
14	C
15	D

Analogies
pp.46–49

1	B
2	D
3	E
4	C
5	F
6	A
7	E
8	A
9	B
10	E
11	F
12	C
13	D
14	B
15	F

Cubes
pp.50–52

1	A
2	B
3	A
4	D
5	B
6	A
7	B
8	C
9	D
10	D
11	D
12	C
13	A
14	A
15	B

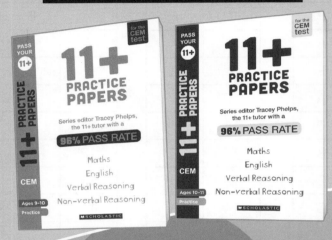

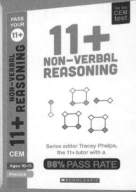